Nectars of Sky

Emerald Crescent, 2000

Also by Michael H. Kew
Crossings (2012)
Rainbownesia (2019)

Nectars of Sky

Verse from the Dipole of Zen Precipice

MICHAEL H. KEW

Copyright © 2020 by Michael H. Kew

All rights reserved.
Published in the United States by Spruce Coast Press.

michaelkew.com
@michael.kew

Library of Congress Cataloging-in-Publication Data
Names: Kew, Michael Hanzlik, 1975—author
Title: Nectars of Sky : Verse from the Dipole of Zen Precipice / Michael H. Kew
Description: First edition. | Brookings, Oregon : Spruce Coast Press, 2020.
Identifiers: LCCN 2020903890 | ISBN 9780997508574 (paperback) | ISBN 9780997508581 (ebook)
Subjects LCSH: Kew, Michael Hanzlik, 1975—American poetry. |
Authors, American—21st century—Nature. | Poetry—Pacific Northwest
LC record available at http://lccn.loc.gov/2020903890

Designed by Sarah Reed
Cover art by Spencer Reynolds
Author photograph by Casie
Landscape photographs by the author

Manufactured in the United States of America
First Edition, March 2020

For Glencora

Contents

Island Mountain 16
Angels of the Arteries 17
White in the Heartwood Night 18
Xeriscapes 21
Womb of Wailaki 22
Two Salmon Creek 23
Trickle of Time Divine 24
The King Range Knot 26
Winter Circle 27
Teardrop Springs 28
The Riot Earth 32
Butterfly Silhouettes 33
Wet Whisper 34
Snowlight in the Kalmiopsis 35
Third Eye of Jupiter 36
Tcet-xo Wolf Moon 38
Blood Vapor 40
Soils of Serenity 41
Diane's Garden 42
The Time We Carry 44
Spell Cosmos 47
Opulence of Sense 48
Redwood Valentine 50
Sky Islands 51
Diamonds of Gaia 52
Saddened Drifts of Meadow Bliss 56
Eve Effervescent 57
Rainbow Arc Toward the Avant-Garde 58
Silence to Sundew 61
Rain in the Afternoon 62
Pickled Babies 63
Mists of Memory 64
Sawdust Iris 65
Salt Sutra 66
Purpleve 67
Psithurism 68
Salmon Sanctuary 69
Pineapple Tranquility 70
Oil Elegant 72
Sanguine 73
Quail Prairie 74
Snaketooth Reverie 75
Saturn Sensorium 76
Cascade Vein of Dream 77
On the Other Side of Air 78

Serendipit   81
New Gale   82
Peace Tears   84
Large Delicious   86
Hook Dreams on the Royal Road   91
In My Blur   92
Magnum Madrone   94
Honeydew   96
Intellictivity   97
Limbic Lightning   98
Mouthfish Mystic   100
Horse Mountain   103
Green Forest Capes   104
Nirvanas of Your Mind   106
Flower Days   107
General Ecstasies   108
Gossamer in Weep   110
Babe Vibrations   111
Empyrean Odyssey   112
Glimpse Dream Eden   114
Fade of Betelgeuse   115
Elk Creek Wash   116
Crystaldrip Camp   119
ForestRe   120
Diesel Honey   121
Drip Meditation   122
Etherealove   123
Dusk Murmur   124
Featheries   126
Five Wick Wick Wick Wick Wick   127
Mellifluous Copulations   128
Cassiopeia's Lullaby   129
Cyclobullience   130
Cry, Cry, Riverbloodingpool   132
Kitty Creek   136
Boughs That Bind   137
Bathluminous   138
Velvet Stardust   140
Candle Magick   142
Babbling Nightbrook of Lady Triptych   143
Zoom to Moon   144
Aurora   146
King Peak Perseus   147
Dreamwood Meridian   149

ONCE THIS WAS ALL BLACK PLASMA & IMAGINATION

—Michael McClure

Island Mountain

often
at my unleashed home elevations
my sole human friends are san diego jazz deejays
spinning from baskets of my proustian musical childhood

smiling cool avant-garde pools for me in which to wet my ears
as a sharp chill settles in over quiet cat whiskers
warm striped orange winter coat
thin ashen cotton

fins of circuit-shorting radiator
boozy montana uncle's oregon square tall glass filled with oatmeal stout
beneath eggwhite donut lamp
chocolate
cocoa
hops

all aside my pubescent stack of intellective beat books
shadows cast over the thankfulness of a smooth oily throat
the night frost creeps
my favorite things
speechless and a-sparkling for 57 and change
secret greeting from the right lane
coltrane tokyo summer '66

that winding snake wizard

radio plays on into the freezewarned night

Angels of the Arteries

enter earth's redwood island
it is shaped like a hopeful letter t
stabbed and scalped all around

sobbed upon by shy capillaries of cloud tears
in stiff tree-bending winds of my quiet riverside reveries
i live to listen to those rushing cloud cobwebs splashing down from all hillsides

stump prairie horse prairie looking-glass prairie yank prairie
wilson prairie high prairie
panda ridge boar backbone devils backbone
palmer butte bosley butte cashner butte morton butte
basin butte pollywog butte snaketooth butte
red mound black mound long ridge short ridge gardner ridge
mount emily
hog mountain?
dead names by dead white times
but

thy misery sky, it bleeds
into the chocolate milk of mother artery
tiny watercapes flayed atop ferns of eternity

press cold whiskers to the furs of red-nosed roses
bulge of black and gray inherit the glass cup of neptune
holy blade music that is blown downslope,
across the burnt diseased waste timbers of venus

White in the Heartwood Night

absorb all glooming withering rags of age,
threshing and thrashing thoughtlessly

how long can they be threadbare and ratty-tat?
how far can one fall when dropped from dropping heavens of suffocation?
wrinkling sagging fraying
slitted eyes and dark circles
wild turkey necks pulverized by the sorrowed slant of southern sleet dreams
mutating to western snow in the blue dusk of all our deaths

all before there lay soft milky white in the winter night
silent flurries hitherto will fly,
fly flishty fairies of ice!
upon the exit of afternoon droopy drip!
in thick fifty knots ocean windy!
dragging along the hard bumpy nails and rusted tracks
clinging to the cold hard bullet train of now

        let's find vibrance in the north
        take the cure of the
        silent silent night snow
        metallurgic bulb of mount emily
        boughs drooping aching white
        on my tongue i catch one flake
        then another
        and out it came as a left-cheek smear
        then another, a tear

quieting the self
always stopping and starting
blowing hot smoke
from desolate stations swallowing fleeting sweat glee
to hard failure
noxious notions of nobody
everlasting nothing

my throbbing eyes train to 150° southeast
facing huge white ranges and imperial conifers
while inside i cry tropical and ancient
outside i beam alone and modern in hopeful dreaming
beeping astray at two hundred thousand miles per grateful hour
                                                            king jerry was right

my dead inner core of vague memories
these crumpling scarlet rags
denouncing time
until the trance of snow
the tao of everything

exhale
        because everything has been nothing
time does not exist to anything but us
depression suppression processes in moshing old winds of that wet whistle
when i wonder if the glass will shatter sleepless soul severity
afternoons of quiet sleeps in rocking black waves
electricities toward dark brown shags of earth
all weights of the world awaiting all that is next
these hurtful sloven rags

all caked with earnest snow of the waning gibbous january moon
look at them whips slip 'twixt my frostbitten fingers
catalytic clustering of foulweather middle-aged sea arches
and sweet spring valleys and white bowls of high forest aimed at sunswept youth

                fairweather fields in the ache of woody heart
                  its tangled roots forever reaching
              digging bending piercing into frozen dreams
                drinking the universe for all else to see
          gasping for golden breath upon four tremorous limbs

                      hairy hardened and alienated
                        scaly mottled aching
                  dehydrated by clouds and lonely wings

railroading branches
melting into mindstorm magna carta winds
ripping at these rotten shreds of doom

pointlessly
eternally
drifting finite straight to infinity
shhhhh
listen to the sweet stillness with muffled ocean roar afar
tiny soft avalanches from branches,
washed by gods of gravity

cold tickle
the silken soothe of snow,
holy crystalline quietude
balm for heavy headached brow
huge cascading galaxies

stars i love you
fall to me
heavenly hexagons of happiness
still
again,
again i cry
like magical silent trees of the divine white

Xeriscapes

warning: empty words from tree
grip strange errors and follow me
drift into the will, and see
cathedral firs lording still
bearfox xylography
visceral black winter topographies
fairytale floral pornographies

xerothermic philosophies of the early fir forest flower
along chemise creek, bear creek, whale gulch creek
calf creek and cow creek and the secret pollens of bull creek
the bee bloom blossoming in eel river beer water
in deep strain of the dry oh dry redwood night

coldface drought about
in defense of dry celestations
desert constellations
bird memory of floods and muds
raindance beneath star skies clogged with crowns

jagged rifts of silken green moss,
i bend a calm ear to the bone
whisper to our sentience
from your soft frontal morningsun glow
to my xerothermic passions
atmospheric river flow
to earth's bone
.....ALOWNE

Womb of Wailaki

old pot murders in these woods,
quiet indeed
missing persons,
chill of winter dews settling into bones buried in firewood canyons

just past dawn the sun jeers the same route,
furling sheets of soft glow upon trunks of the old-growth tanoak in the side length
light wind rush of cold dead leaf morning acorns
stringy dense whisker thickets
lazy rains preclude cloudsdrift from the northwest,
smothering the blue
snagged by rich mountaintops,

my friends, ensnare
saddle mountain horse mountain
bushy blue squirrels and manzanita whitebells
soft big flat air, the hazy horizon lays in ripples of cobalt
the ridge blue blue ridge razorbacks finding the buzz of bees and madrone trees

all grown up to block your weary teary vistacrisp eye

Two Salmon Creek
for Laura

fungi hippie yogini nymph in coffeecot blue pelt
moony round rims and stringbean belt
thin blonde sacrum hair
an undulating artiste
warmwhip your whittled dews
splash your smile onto whorled heartsick views

i too smile and glean your angelic dance over the fairy glen
praising old humble brownwood bridge
the scent of rogue-siskiyou forest tars
fresh rains
cenozoic redwood in far domino ridge

learn learn learn kiss all every swordfern
clap and plumb salmonberry falls
beneath the ancient stream of strain
lean into ignorant orange chainsaws
into stoic island drainages
'twixt stump field
fragrant myrtlewood
diesel road
holy jade river

shut your slitted eyes in the
fern grotto dreamings of clover banks
blurry black whiting world stirs anew
we can find a million solaces in old worlds preserved
touch the teachings of fungal fecundity
retrace the sad battles in vertical braille

Trickle of Time Divine

heavy brine iodine claws at the fat wuthering alluvial fan
fertile steppe of black loam
indian willow grove culled by northswell and boxy odious homes and diesel boat fry
upward to dry chemise and chaparral
the same soapy blacksand scent and sight of holy shorepound and rude
death drownings
also,
beat farm tractors dragging beat boats in and out of the beat shark sea

oh, old kenny v
i saw you
heard you have prostate cancer
old friend
fishing heart bless
your peppersalt beard dips into quiet plateaus and the endless wind
rocks shelves scoured rough

rolling slow spray gentle fierceness
lurching over ancient abalone civilizations facing the rippling weeds
and the old quivering grasses
seasonal shear as the clouds creep in and birds fly north

and still i gaze out into the gray serration dream about lingcod-filled coolers
and quiet happy days drifting deeper into cerebral isolation
black shrapnel of seabirds in oval flights low over the chop
as tiny headwind airplane circles to land
in the quantum leap of mankind in the making

old grudges
new earths

heart witherings and reliefs
of time healing and deleting
let's remember the whoosh of transcendence to pierce optimistic infinities
and lure cannabis farmers from texas

who reap sound baths of exotica from asian descents
dreaming of counterfeit cash and
chocolate coffee
here in the nexus of green and once greed sense
shelter cove, at last
i eye you anew

20
2000
2020

drier taller sweeter deeper
bust boom bust boom swoon
i cry outwardly
inwardly i see clearly
hoot! faith!
naturally
hidden manifest echo of youth
hidden manifest trickle
hidden bright trickle of the time
hidden lost coast
is divine

The King Range Knot

                    keep out!
                 private property!
          immense long green and brown fences
                 shut from galaxies
     no trespassing into the junked school buses and pickups
            ancient little mailboxes looking new,
and the pencils of douglasfirmadronetanoak 'cross the huge cow valley
                into the king oh king
            my king of man, that of which made me

        wilder ridge road, many unknown homes and steads,
              king peak road, landscape dry february
              cooskie mountain, lord of southrainfall
  mini bell boxes mini secretive gates and fences avoiding human squall
            concealing great queendom cannabis secrets
      ettersburg road looking across to saddle mountain and fire hill,
    north fork bear creek scintillazing between rocks into the trees

                 oh, clear as her teasing me
              ancient seeps in the jagged gravel road
                   which is hardly a road
         large beautiful firms that look like three furnaces,
           babbling brook down to the bearcreek car scraped
              four-wheel-drive to tranquil riverwinds
                in the remote horse mountain lee
          among deadbone drycrisp feather rills of tanoak
                   flitters of a dirt floor a-full

                      yes—unseasonal
              as seen through eyes aged twenty years
     huckleberry sweetly suckling on madrone mothers and fathers
                   twisted kin of indian winter

Winter Circle

drape old zinvines 'round green glass of heart
squeeze tired liver into warm bright snow moon of monday
tides really swinging now,
hey!
spindrift flurries soak surfing gulls
zenblind of early day

Teardrop Springs

        cute flared cup of quaint rockered sportvision,
swerving pushing mashing into deep fortitude of that soaking rain shatter
where does it take us?
dory boat redone
high prow—dream now
rogue river dna

                      there is no permanent self
                      do not worry for death
        creep downstream unrecognized in the airs of evolution
              little brittle oars like black wasp antennae
                  predation sedation in the early orblight
                  warm from january night drumroll squall
                      it all ends in full bellies

feel that cold of hull and plug in
cortex fears
impossible
never never know in the reeds of strangelove
the water may mirror minds of murder

windless
winless
atomic infinities
lettus float down into today's history
always yes, always a fish mystery
not one glass bowl to spit in
        man abusing the abused
leisure long past luxurious sustaining life rhythms
spiritual energies
systems soulful yet sinister to the unnatural order
lazy sad pastel mists blossom to salvation of abused woods
mashed and beaten and poisoned for poverty
all once of ash
        and again
and old beards old lard old cold men of white

kill everything quickly
our world slows so swiftly
fixate on seams and whitewaters
        and winter idiom
divine world always
thrashing winds may appease you
everything is always older
declines in attitude flattened by forced four-finger flings
negative capabilities adhere to ignorance

slickening oily bluey-green fingers into wet dip wine minds and whiskey woes
drooping gloop glotty gurgle burble undulating tows sweep quiet cobbles shift
but not for the death of beautiful hens
salmon peaceful slink hidden in ice-rockriffle greens
thrash into wide awkward net so we can hold you dead laughing in the sun sparkles
trophy days of digital doom
ensure it fits into the frame for facebook praise
the riffles below serrated clearcutted bend rod

      scarred brown bare hillsides return to prairie roots pre-plantations
                  peer into spider eddies
                aqua acid prisms swirl inertia
          tiny barb invasive spoiling what's been spoiled
                    no worry for tomorrow
                burnt cigarette of yesterday
                  broken glass politics
                    withstand poison
                        can you?

i'm thinking about yellow lenses
heavy rains yes you may unlock the door
desaturate the ego
sleep to heavy shower
when the wind and rain dies we can hear the distant dogs and roosters
philosophical pebbly septic dirt of fertility
smell the exit to entrance

                in trance
                   why?
      fluidity is the real gold of sentience
        the rains, they reason with you
  they pound our thin bone temples and roofs of cowardice

eons of now
of flashes from fruits of sperm

pale rocky shore of stripped burn-outs in lightbulbs of old earth
vale visions of hollow winds and offshore moaning whistle buoys
chasing us all inland to fresh fresh freshwater
i wove past at forty

maybe fortyfive or fifty
fleeing
needing
hangovers of fern

                tiptoe to the far bank and glass the earth
                  the old gangsters of grassy glen
                      gaiety immense

                      just wait till spring
                              no!
                          nothing

windbreeze soft forever falling west southwest eternal inertia of life force
our skinny hopeful barbs reach over one another passing serenities of gentle jade
of mossyrock
                                              wild rivers?

      not so wild
tranquil pursuit old time no motor no smoke no smell no noise
drift
believe

best to leave it all alone
catch and release
fish torture
little rainbows flit from the sunny
gurpling guppy brooks

happy hollow howls
whiskered jowls
the orange cat grinds his red gums
on your pink evenflow of stressed salmonid night

The Riot Earth

rowdy north coldmetal wind
josts and jigs the riverbank fluff
bushy verdant walls of bliss
mother's trees juicing in slow-motion

warp of wood
dark evergreens sharpening to
soft dainty-fresh alders and myrtle
all scheming for fertile sun from that clear eye of sky

waters too will bamboozle the color wheel
from the soft gin blues of pools, lazy-swirled with brown mouse eddies
somnolence in blurred reflections of this earth-riot

and so we slide between its sands
packed firm coarse gray and countless bright
winterwashed with jade greatness funneled from afar
birthed deeply cool in the kalmiopsis
fertilizing everything
as all remnant wilds will do

Butterfly Silhouettes

                                                                let's talk about that bottle again

it's not a battle

                                                                                         it's a bottle

bottle of what?

                                                                          bottle of whom?

can we plug a bottle atop this beauty?

                                                       the word 'bottle' annoys me

just let the conifers groan

                            perving on seamy steamy streamy creeks

squawking drainages of our dirty minds

                                                              and so still we sit

and the longer we wait

                    nuthatches will resume their holy chitter chat

Wet Whisper

coyly cunningly creepy chanterelle!
                         you creepy slimy little umbrella
flaunting your scrumptious meat woodsworth woodiness
       with your infinitely lovely name
orangeyellow quivering dirt blob hides in your needle shade of creeks to ponds
to fir plantations
we are looking
                in gentle old preserved forage of raw greens in rivervalley rains
slime my fingers while i fondle yours
       droopy hard wings, wet fungi dreams
try to scrape dirtflecks and sad fir needles from your flowery cape
           whisper
      beneath heavy skeletons of snow-wary shadow

intrusive late sun
goodbye for now?

                     nay!

      fueled cats unfooled
          bean-leaping over skynectars pooled
 in forever pebbly weedy septic muds
cooled

      all this inside specimen days placed centrally within the catnip of winter
for the quiet deer families freed from gunshot greed
      intricacies of the midday lamplight eye
           a kind soft quiet hush of raw winter boomjams up the north-forking fronting overdue aleutian juicing

yes yes
spiky fir airs fry spackling
          now we oil up and

      FUNGI FEAST
                          in communist white rice!

Snowlight in the Kalmiopsis

botanical jewelbox of backlight glisten

listen

to the
driplight blind midwinter of sundew
to the

lifting low laugh of the
painted lichens

inhale
the
burning shadow piney prisms of tears
inside tiny shy avalanches from droopy boughs of treebone

tanoak tinkly
sprucey shimmer
magicly manzanitas

darlingtonias and madroneys
yes you too dream in the freeze
but here with
melting vapor, my eyes are open
here, lover
to hear the calm zenracket of raining trees

Third Eye of Jupiter

    above squat voluptuous bottom-heavy doug fir in meadow bosoms
    my hindu lunatic zen goddess levitates in the south midsummer sky

        embedded deep inside the milky way naval
        hovering atop the klamath mountains
        where jupiter is my goddess's golden third eye

            weeks later
            i redream the scene
                as
                 C
                 Y
                 C
                 L
              O O O
                 P
                 S

            eye-vibe antithesis
        nightmare of evil rude pampas grass
           bushy pale featherheads

crowding the creeks
cutting streaks
razorwhip tentacles

        my ears flush to a lone hopeful grass cricket
           my eyes oil to an awaiting sea
           my comforting cold seam of gray

           all stars are christmas lights
             all greenyred twinkle
        shooting and scooting and falling
       all small and big and countless and strange

                  black holes
            comforting constellations
                  early still
    rippling snake of fog ocean snuffs the river valley

                  and later—

                  zodiacal light

                                    long sundew in the west
                                    harvestmoonless night
                                         late september
                                                    so

                                                and so
                                i lick sweet poems of raindrops

Tcet-xo Wolf Moon

                  howling meowing pebblesoft sandness
                              of hard
shifting surfy fullmoon riversand rain crust creating wondrous waves
                louded unseen prenumbral lunar eclipse

                                                              the three of us!
                                                               gemini twins
                                                                 cancer crab
                                                         so so nice to see you!

again

                                     yet yet yet i blur low into toward you
             your yearly scallop bay intrusions in normal steep severity of surf suds
                                           jetty rocks unknowing unmoving uncaring
                                                         anything for down
                  heavy white boats pass us all in old slow stinky diesel exhaust

wild viticulture freejazzing into cold loud gray southwestwind
tailing the brighting stars of northwind yore
woodwinds affixing to my mindweb of monthlong ocean detox

                                                                     purple nectar
                                                     it shall unclog galaxies
                                     it shall be slow slumberous sugarbricks
                           and scented candles to infuse indigo absorption

fountainspring of youth
naturally we all love you and you
your happy bearded loaded crab pots crab boats all entwined in pathetic archaic ether
obesity and insanity to all end

and it will

                        for now yes yes we shall fetch you all later
for now it is unknown whether the weather will stand or fall to gale and bop squall
                                       for now we are loaded
                  for now your beard smokes past you in sandy rarity

for now windchill of wednesdays wanting
for now wines in windy twilight sweats of loneliness
for now my reflexing meat saga sags in cold sweetness
for now this was all awaiting everything

                howling weeping meowing creeping beeping sighing crying
                              old gray smoky lens upon us all
                    old tired midwinter depressions in the fat of wind
           breaking those buoys and blinding those boomblasting black birds

the sea it does roar roar roar and roar
southwestwind please slap me
sacred cancer crab
for now, for us, please please please shut your salted moony moneytrap door

Blood Vapor

                fractalingling sun in moist clearing eyes of ice
          canceling the long silent blacking drip of cold weird-ass night
                      arc into old leaves of white glare
                  tap three thin squawky beeps of nuthatch
                      jazzjiving with jays and juveniles

        stand up and let's forage elsewhere in the yellow fields of DNA

turkeys slaughtered
pigs bled
unthankful
ovens hot
sopped meat
                      old bloods of young promise
                      man toasts brutality of man

                          how do YOU feel?

Soils of Serenity

                      THIS is an infant symbol

                                          fragment of space
                                                  and TIME

                                                      which is not
                              when i get to share these colors

                                                  in these regions
                    at the stairway we see exhalations in inhalations

                      mycorrhizae

each tree is more than any of us combined

                            WILL
                                EVER
                        BE

                        quiet!
                  hear that bird flyover
       roll yourself up and let the dirt take your feathers
    bake your fur

look at the shadows

                                        look at these worlds inverted

these whirling and driving and floating and
                            your wavering death of autumn is coming

everything is smog

                          HONEST BEAUTY

Diane's Garden

what's beyond that gate? off to the right?
oh, just a grower
older lady
(older than me)

some might call her an apple-eyed hippie
'60s residual
she just wants to be left

A
L
O
N
E

and so in autumn weeks on we went
diane and me—
'twixt pensive walls of rain in the heavens of the lost coast night
tip-toeing down the steep long wooded gulch to bucolic horse mountain reefs

in my old ripped yellow shorts and with shaggy blond ponytail
left arm gripping brian kang tri-fin (later destroyed by airline)
private waves in jumping green sweetwater seas

i watched as in black sand you hunched for jewelry gems
below our dual sanctuaries on dual high
duly clung to old precarious cliff kaluna
beneath lullabies of sweetsunned manzanita

dusty bumpers and back windows
needless generator purr
off-grid abundance adhered from society
forests of pre-legal cannabis dreaming in white fabric cocoons
later trimmed with stickyfingers by candlelight
into dawn conversations amid ferny wallpaper and woodburn crackle

hokusai great wave frame behind your bony faux wood table
your shimmering freelove tales unforgotten
floating there above our emerald crescent
high windy hill swoop of bear and bald eagle,
fogs below, fires above—

lost undulations beneath cirrus skids
diamonds among dews of desolation
ah, diane
self-identified floozy of yore
gardening, meditating, yogaing, zenning at the green king peak gate
living your best life yet

soft cherubic smile
flower dress and kashmir sweat
soulful eyes of opal age
all cosmologic crystal ball and bohemian hats

diane,
please ear me

if you're breathing, i wish you're not alone as we both were
cleaved by generational gaps
and i never ever got to say goodbye
to your sovereign golden honeydew waves of wisdom

at that strange end to our short rainbow dance

The Time We Carry

        i once carried a white single-fin
            black dry-bag

   tick-blocking pants and day-hikers
   clomp through a shady hall of maple
              alder
            blackberry
              salal
              thistle
           poison oak
                      —(ONLY TO US)
              ferns,
        wind-sheared sitka
     down to this gap in the coast
              rocky
              reefy

           warmcalm sunday—
drought inland forestfire haze mutes the great yellow orb
 soft-focus pastels blur cirrus into psychedelic sea
         orange mirror of summer
  dreamtime polarity of currents and constellations

    look: gulls and seals and a spouting whale
      bobbing bull kelp lazing in the drift
    swaying with the surge of empty cages
      laced white with ribbons of rage

                SEA
                 P
                 L
                 A
                 S
                 M
                 A

coldly fragrant-fresh deep jade!
matches the hillside groves
air of salt and soot
seastacks and tortured rocks
relics of a coast a billion years young

i lurch behind 60,000 years of human pollination to reach this beach
primordial panorama
beige strip of heavily driftwooded sand
course like cracked pepper
lorded by woods and seacliffs

by you i am unseen
publicly private
ephemeral refuge
church of open sky

i could be elsewhere

since middle paleolithic horn of africa
we've walked
we've carried things
pelt quiver for arrows

eye for the east
pilgrims scattered

woven dreams
OF ZEN PRESENT
in ethiopia
FUTURE PAST

threading middle east and silk road
fording bering sea
descending the americas to tierra del fuego—man's omega

four-p.m. sun balms my face
i watch the creep of tide, the diurnal teaser,
        the sandbar-drownerdowner
                the surf was fleeting, now dead

LIKE US

93 percent of all humanity to ever live
more than 100 billion
gone
GONE

soul vapor
bone dust
atomic reincarnation?

five ospreys squeak and twirl
fish too will die
ancient circle
wheel of life

i stand and shoulder the bag
see unknown colors
step from past to present
foyer of forest
discovering it again
supplanting memory
carrying things
one age to the next

closer

(closer to now)

Spell Cosmos

                                        the cold world looks warm
                                                              in
            purple
                                    sit here and meditate on
           purpleness
                                                        my
            purple
                                                    face
                                                    my
            purple
                                                  jeans
                                                   my
            purply
                                      genie gobbledygook
                                    in the blisses of bliss shades
                                as the sun cooks salt into my
            purple
                                               pores
                                           star matter
                                           soon come?
                                           where the
            purple
                                        parties were
                                               sun
            purplepurple
                                               KIN
                                                 of
            purple
                                                 sin

Opulence of Sense

we like to see our lives warmer
but cool is cool

we like to see
everyone else's lives
in the fields of what he or she was given
color blindness of oneself

earth is orange
earth is purple
earth is twittering bluegreen croaking crows
tinkle of insects in rhododendron rush

who is wondering?
the wing beats
the wings boot
twitter
no-sweater weather

insects furious
wind loud
in truck we wait

weave
raise
flow
do a tour

between madness
twerp in twilight
torpid and purple highlight
the shadows receding
those planets
as i watch you eat
you forage
YOU FORAGE!

who shall say anything against?

the thorns we want to prick
like the souls in those blazing blazing whitecaps
that searing searing golden ocean of oceans
reset and wonder why are we all on this machinery
no hard heart here

we can see buttered minds across the scattered scapes
ether earth belowfeet
i can see them—
sink needles into glass bulbs

Redwood Valentine
for Michelle

                late-night mad poetry readings and ruminations

chuck berry tapes and indian incense
cheap bourbon and local stout beer

cat dog salt and sandy sheets

                  on the instance of indian winter summer
                        the redwood cabin
                      love is a muddy pathway uphill
                              yes

       love is the morning sun down the lonely hot heart of hope and —

                                                     and?

Sky Islands

by daybreak?

the gorgeous act lay

N
A
K
E
D

deflated tanoaks and firs and myrtles
alder fatalities
fluent floods
slaughter slides
raw chocolate rivers
ocean swell trains huge
all gutted by gales
yes, my sky exhales
brow furrows

surf day?
no
no

N
O

none of these for a winter wit

Diamonds of Gaia

we could always kiss while soulsearching for northernmost native coastal redwoods in the dirt faces scarred and newtonian, grimacing browntoothed chins of archaic ignorance on down deep into the autumn oregon night,

we could kiss dry crack-lipped cracking slacking on through waxing skins of young february snows atop deep intrusive advertised veinery of central coasts near millions of those hungry summer seekers far far out in conditioned weaves of lifetimes huddled muddled crying to flee but still can never agree,

we could kiss watching the neon light industrial chic of windy waters slipping down doublepane glass into old carrot muds and rhododendron deadwoods of the january night,

we could kiss between two of the most beautiful english words—red wine— and gaze upon eastern views of kansas and kathmandu while wondering where there to all the wine flows and to whom and to why while red minds fly white way back across the insane afternoon's quiet space shuttles of intersectionality so we can again get drink-drunk across the raw plains of memory and avail awkward glances that tow tenderness yet never gloss over our bruised wandering broken hearts,

we could kiss while patting happy dogs over hard sands in the rainy dusk of depression and deceit and bundled bohemia that for both of us rang deep and warm and true and earth's heritage finally honored your furry beige fur-boots and exquisite glasses above that pillowy shawl below your big white teeth of purity,

we could kiss into wet-shirt obnoxious portland pulse nights of downtown stained-rug brown motel from wetblack hours of driving while arguing and negotiating your gentle curious insanities and cat-killings and acid-washed cortexes of softness and breathe way beyond the nightmares of emergency rooms,

we could kiss as i seduce you on these sunny december sands indeed amongst flat noodles of bloodshot eyes, audacity of hot split summers and no snows while all the while you could realize that in the end you would do it all again and again,

yes!

    we could kiss while you late-night winedrunkenly classify me as 'trouble' and we take long expensive winter road trips north, always north, and one time we took a jet aeroplane into rare snows of my heartical sprout and we bickered and brow-bashed and drank warm beer in scotch hangovers at the rocky shelter cove seaside both wishing we were both there with somebody else,

    we could kiss after i remark to your good rich friend about her 'dancer body' and she vows never again to introduce me to another of her blonde soul sisters because two of them were sly shy goddesses in the shot-blue dry eyes of a desperate searchlight of validation premature and yet there we were in those misty gray summer wonders of photographic odysseys,

    we could kiss while you pervert my toilsome tiny films of old micronesia as i admire your newly tanned exposed belly-button above your hippiegirl string rope belt and blue bell-bottoms well below your young hungry starry blue-eye jade jeweled desert enthusiasms and soon we will have beers and tacos and you suggest massages and you pause for a mind of intent and lonely rurality yet chosen in avoidance of stained dawns and crackly bulb radios in the ear of leaf-blowers and farm tractors and pre-dawn garbage trucks and evil bald neighbors with aggressive large brown dogs piercing to annoy all within earshot on schedule of constants,

    we could kiss while we surf into sunset down the cute lane from my collegiate confusions and bend ears to sade and chat about stressful urban nights and obvious rejections and regret into ideals of blondblonde surfnicity in seas of sedation and the antisolitude of dogbark beaches below the scratchiness entwined with atmospheric aggressions of impossibly huge red lighthouses upon rocks upon wool socks upon our warped warmth of innocence,

    we could kiss into dawns of drunk stained saggy couches upon the independence day constellations infused with impromptu live reggae dance while our friend farts and mentally films our summerheat frolickations and i ask you about russia and your horses in colorado and the one time i again see you, you widen the brown eyes of my slippery roommate of generosity, bless him and those ripping showers of flighty hecticity and wrinkled wet-bar flirtation hands in the face of sailors and fishers and head-pounding pours for the non-poor, we could kiss upon your midwestern lifeguard red one-piece large-breast bad-breath interest in greenland in the beachside bar as i recall our first meeting out years prior at that glary sparkly windy oceanbeach below hard eyes of commerce wondering where the birds flew off to and why the air still smellt of tar, but then we drink enough and more and sometimes drive in your small white truck of even more reggae of those early days and you are shunned by the dumb wolf of water street, and the time we meet once more i flatten myself sad-drunk on the sticky fat nightclub floor amid blissy sweaty glowsticks of smiles,

we could kiss after sinking illegal lemon vodkas after you email me from the strange legal blue ether and you goldenvoice your sweet barely legal barbie doll insanities and you tell truths of broken glass sermons in semens of serenity, or so you wished now, silent in your padded cell,

we could kiss after meeting on the windswept grass at the ocean in the flower noon glare while your mother gazes into earthquakes of evil that indeed paved the pathway over fatal optimism, the green muddy mandala that fell into the rough fishy lost seashore, and then you might invite me thousands of miles eastward to high crags of confusion and white weddings and perfect tranquil green fruit valleys of sun that yawn below the prettiest peaks of primordialism imaginable and i sleep in your hot blue truck in that tiny sparkling mountain mining town while wondering why our starry vernal twinkles had been swept away,

we could kiss in sun-soaked floridian vapors as you wheel your cracked white rubber along the sea with your uncertain antennae of eternity balling that jack across asphalt and the wrathy wines of napa, finding no gold in gold beach but dramatic diamonds in delirium,

we could kiss in a blind candleshower from taxicabs of rain and february darks in all confused blur with insane talks of liquid sheets to the wet black dawn of an unknown equinox,

we could kiss amid gray rock delusions momentous of recent indignation and shame after months of shadows between here and there and you cigarette-strut your bleached shady stripper whims across my cold evening porch in fogs of lap-dances and cheap sweet midwest bottled beer and spontaneous philosophy on photography and the sad deep cry of your nicotine mind abused in passing afore drug haze amassing,

we could kiss that one pastel orange-gray afternoon across the righteous fields of academia, you in your orange-gray african skirt and olive skin and secretive brown eyes and velvet smile as alien to her purse that gave you away in the end in the tiny blue car parked at my yellow flat at the greedy north face of care where you would cry to me quietly through crackly wires and loud bubbling finnish hot tub steams and hotels of cars in the wailaki woods before the weak ecstasy in yellow meadows and sun-warmed black beach river rocks buried you in your books of distractions and interventions and aimless intentions,

we could kiss while the one-armed jughead lay at bay clueless and you asked me about camping and ancient energy and masturbation and in theory there were more camping trips and more sade / 'sex music' and always there were cats in the corner of my maroon corduroy organic hemp pants while we sipped ale and your black hooker leggings drew stares from the old drunks in the dim brown downtown brewery where your fieriness for waves and woods and warlocks rose to a pitch as we drained pitchers of red nectar and oatmeal stout,

we could kiss after subdued cyber calls led into hazy late-night dubby booze-sweat soak-shirt eureka dancenights so we can hangover in cloudy bay brutality eyed by your parents cusping on heavenly solo cloudless weekends at the rustic big lagoon cabin in quietude of ultimate redwood coast trinidad tea café coziness and yet never again would i see you past the forts of bragg,

we could kiss finally yes at last through your dazzling heterochromia eyes in the skid row greasy snows of old west seattle upon the lark of communal fogs, driving in the cold night along the dark strait and rounding out over there, hooked in the aquatic concrete earth luring us into dark cigarette cedar dens of flannel grunge and skull-grip vices that everybody will regret if they can simply recall and recite the ice of time and the tempests and endless endless endless temptations of—

Saddened Drifts of Meadow Bliss

oh, how i have waited for these trancelike white dawns
oh, how i have baited gods with spiced goods now gone
upon mournful dreams i walked and met clefts
crept to the crunch of surprised silent depths

i stepped onto brown-ringed porkpie stumps
where my sorrows eternal vowed to stay clumped,
i dragged among oregon blackberry veins of ice water
i stood and reimagined the onion of my life,
hey son hey daughter
tender daydreams of imaginary diamond-mist wife

anxious i awaken beneath midnight light-flashes
power lines now fierce, dipping drooped in deep meadow snows
alone i walked ahead of that morning's dim ring,
all brilliant cougar and bear and twelve-point knows
alone i walked with reverie—my one soulmate

and once there were phantom magic white poofs cascading,
once there were big bears and old sawdusts
once there were great woods long scalped to slash
imminent surrendering to snow chain tracks

hello sad-eyed kitty, taste holy smoke in a glass
hello stormy long seam of lonesome ocean unsnowing

you too shall pass

Eve Effervescent

gusts start and startle
each cusp a low hiss
deep breath drawn
hold it!
DEEPER
fifteen miles an
HOUR

to twenty
to twenty-five
to thirty-five
forty to forty-five
to fifty
to sixty
seventy

topping seventy-nine
before again inhale
i exhale because
no one i know can find me

HERE

Rainbow Arc Toward the Avant-Garde

three duplicate blackwhite cats fly dying
shining
three young monks in fatty warm shiny sheaths
tuxedos of softness
sharpdressed all for all death
as all of us be and be

churning of frostnight swivels bleed clouds beneath mean headbright moon
let us take a very strange walk down
to feed fresh kale to the yellow hens
for lunch we must eat sleet
gassing into morning glare of leftovers
crashing ping cymbals blessed blend with tooting bop horn
hushing rainstreams all beneath the wet red sorrows of dirt winterday

why do snowflakes unstick?
why?
ask old joe

all of us spin and stretch in heavy flannel gray jeans while the curious new sun
clamps all across drizzly damp camps of sunburnt bums dreaming about free hot
coffees and oily raw white beat wheels promising old sun and heavy smiling eyes
dripping their own hot wax of soul candles that can never be smoked

no matter
shapeshifttt
my island
meadow and woods as ocean
blue lake of morning
gurgling wintercreeks succumb to the burgling of bombastic birds who know
       brightly where they fly,
soaring soddenly short of these regroupings and loopings of all sanities well-worn
       into the freedom of clearcuts

propagandic poison
plastic pool-roofed greenhouse in glorious glary grays of the oregon afternoon

greens gushing toward springtide splendors
resisting into wet-nosed tight-bow stampstomp violin drumbeats

wavy thinning wet hairs
each a ping of clarity of knotted fir and pebbly red drainages of manzanita and pine

scratch the temples and wander into the tinkly bouncy tenorman dusk
haunt the hideaway of hens
gustoficous glorious radar of cougar and bear
drips of january evolving to clear flat little dirt-track waves of innocence as for eons
        every one of us has seen before we were born

once we all had the same view
once we shall all again
once i walk unplanned into the sweetness of afternoon between storms of serenity
once wet glistening salal solitude

dribbling into swordfern sanctuary
past two froggy clear algae-faced ponds
past sad mossy trunks of impatience

you are all invited
once everything means nothing
everything remains brow-beaten down brown far from town

yes,
up here you can close your minds to eight artworks
all from birth and outline vibes of orange
all of this is a hangover of a hangover distilled by birds bees and blooms and gods in
        the glass sky
slamming into erotic rocks weaving and keying and tink-tattling over and over over
        comfortable beneath modern heat

and so
and so we wait
we wait again

look west
'where is your moon?' the funny bum asks me
if only it could pierce the wandering radiances and squirty reed choruses
paean to spontaneous paths
the old cold dusty wallpapers of iris and herb

listen—deep bass drum echo
bong gurgle yet again
take another look at these wet wildroots
temple-scratch
dehydrate
thrumb drum to bass trumpets
we all remain static
standstill

greased wheezy weepy windowsill whiteness
clink and thrum along into the halfmoon meaningless crossfires
drumming into rare happysad snowdrifts of the mid-january black cat night
subconsciously where i see frostbitten rainbows in zinfandel threes

chirp your echoing flute sharp pattertap brass
shatter into the old green oregon of hopeful holy

                                        hermitage

Silence to Sundew

raw dawn saturday depression
in cold winter mountain house
alone
always alone

soft pitterpatter of remnant storm
black purring cat warm soft at my right bow
sunrise at another white blue gray
head into another throb
more winehaze
milky masked skin clammy sticky

hateful

no

pity

no

no magic of running fresh water
to wash it all away
to restore my smile
to make anew
my sunny fermented limbic rucksack

smile smile smile
self-care
yes you i do love

Rain in the Afternoon

oh once i went looking for earth's northernmost natural 21st century coast redwood
grove
yeah
right down there
but

rain resumed
daylight dimmed
sweating and slippage amongst ferns and huckle leaves
dusk and hungerings
dark mozart earbud sonataings
gaped on me back to town for a mcdonald's nonfoody combo #1
big mac medium fries medium drink

on his mobility scooter at the next table 'twas retired logger
beatific
drinking free coffee and reading newspaper
looked over and wondered aloud why me splattered with dried mud

'yeah we used to pull a lot of redwood out of there'
gargle-voiced

'not many of 'em left

is that right?'

those fries?

much too salty

Pickled Babies
for Sarah

> well the sun is out
> with no hint of snow
>
> in other news,
> everyone can relax because
> i bought more scotch
> for the healthy development of
> our second child
>
> wine the amniotic fluid
>
> the womb a sack
>
> of booze with baby
> pickling
>
> sarah—can you feel it?

Mists of Memory

rain quiets all ambience of change
of introspection
of carnal chaos

WHOOSH

the rain is singular yet
angles
intensity

voracity

sound

speed
swooping in from the gray over-ocean blurs
hard fogs
cyclical

wall of wet of infinity drawing near,
its origin thousands of miles out
in turbulent brain patterns

pure peaks of happy wilderness
that yes you can climb

Sawdust Iris
for Spencer

vogue outerworld
oregon innerworld
a boy in chetco
wet coastal bump

huge swells
rocks
many waters
angler's eden

he doesn't fish
he paints
sometimes in his sylvan hillside studio
sometimes in his clean midtown gallery
sometimes atop a scenic glen amid spruce and spindrift

the coast that cast him away
lifetimes later he returned
for life

for family
natal homing
like salmon to his holy dear

Salt Sutra

                    storm coast crying wet motion
                           and emotion
             dark gray hours upon fullmoon black fogs
toxic steam rising from dirty mill stacks upon the town's rock shoulders
                hairy hands yanking cheap beer taps

soak thy floors with piss

dumb farting beer-belly log trucks bullying the blurred diesel air
bumbling down from huge abused hills and hollows where
        rude greasy orange banshee chains chew through nature's hope
slanted rain shimmering and sheeting across avenues
cursed trees wrestling, gale-bent
i watch through cold double-pane windows
down which
the gravity-ooze of rain smears into

newbreathing mouths of rivers and creeks
blown out into the brown indifferent pacific where
gulls surf along and above and along these high aleutian swells
bashing primordial high sheer universe rock
loud gulls
charmed beings
                                                    iloveyou
shrieking and squawkingly smoothgraceful
soaring in roaring updrafts after streaking
along gray hugetops of near-lurching white lips
then wing-arcing up

                          your dance

                          is forever

Purpleve

smudgy reflection of refraction glasses
bending light
rainbows shooting from sun
like fissile missiles of rainbows,
creaks in the trees
from birds
from bees
misted looming foggy forest in sunlight
blankets and glowing, baby turned out well
flashy hairy fairy flowers and
hazy daisies and cats creeping
little boxes of prisms
promises of peace
of reds and yellows
of blues and greens
of purples

PURPLE

everything is

N
I   B
A   O
R   W

Psithurism

as i openeye to sundown cool
i spy green candycane weeds restored as miniature green swords
the cats think i've gone mad
suddenly,
in the mute of sunset
they've become giants
if you stare at something long enough
you can make it into what you want it to be
or

it will show you what it needs to be

hollow voices
branches of fir
like fingertips
tinkling
tickling
the air

the tree is a heart
open to the north fork canyon
the horizon throbs magenta and blue
earth tones
faded heathers
first nation raven from the far north scolded me

silhouettes of the long-ago serrated spines
bled off to the infinity of insanity

Salmon Sanctuary

genie
i see you
invisible spirit
dancing
dancing in the smoke of the trees
you jive to the ravens
their wingbeats
featherleaves
pointing the way to you in this blur
this pulsing
heating
scintillating
sparkling
warm orange and yellow
purple
pink
celestial salmon run
reveries of slipstream bliss

Pineapple Tranquility

huge kaua'ian cloud forefinger
pointed straight at me
aloha state, deep wet hawai'ian kiss

you three thousand miles of moisture
northeast pacific-spanning
breeding sheeting subtropically bleeding

                                                                   R
                                                  A
                                          I
                            N

smoldering boiling bouldering
steaming through canyons in from the monotone
mute fog-gray haze of hawai'i
of garden isles

shearing the visibility
power-washing the groves of old sitka
live color looking grayscale

from house i walk wet
the earth shiny like fish scales
the gravel-crackle of rain pellets pelting my hairy hooded head
i hear the sea

a happy distressed mess of shredded gray
aggressive alaskan gulf groundswell
flecked in jagged whites and spinning lumps

impressing black storm-sculpted rocks
depressing black dead-looking trees
defenseless!

BLASTroar of surf
SWEAT ELIXIR
like close-proximity to an interstate
all amplified by subwoofers of wind

sassy sizzle across the grumpy grass
these coastal woods swaying drunkenly to and fro
limbs heavy

bending and flapping
fat raindrops
come home, bee

                YOU ARE DAYDRUNK

                     mahalo!

Oil Elegant

fly with me, swishy birds
swishy-wing with me
what is this galloping?
what are we shivering for?

nothing to shiver
nothing to say
i have lubricant
the air is clear

trapped in your brain
are instincts
every tentacle
every fiber
do you hear this clarity?
do you feel my greasy brain?

that blue searing sucking horizon?
NOW i see who you are

Sanguine

narrow coastal strip
curry to monterey
earth's tallest living organisms
once
coated
more
than
two
m
i
l
l
i
o
n
acres
gold rush
white human flock
miners
wrecked rivers
sawmills
chewed trees
five percent left
ninety-five percent death

Quail Prairie

sadness was sheared from false soul of summer
sadness was unleashed to range wild face of panic
sadness of mind awareness was flat-pinned to snowdrifts
sadness, insane wee hour dreams of tropical scotland and perfect peregrinations
sadness that screams long 'cross burnt fields of freedom
sadness of clogged cortex and deep dives down the raped mound of serenity
sadness shedding storm nights and meditation days
sadness melting to warmth beneath wiry musical magenta falls
sadness bleeding oaky fruit heart to unfeeling time
sadness and past happiness, oh, it will be a-changing
sadness, so i peel from the middle-aged flames of crises
sadness, blinding exposures through swing-doors of imperception
sadness, nothing dies down there
sadness, everything lies above

Snaketooth Reverie

redwood
i've seen you
why should i even save you?
or me?
or you again?
or him?

there about those with them?
to what do i speak at all?
speak like a child
expose your emotions
expose your raw fertility

expose your origins
expose your shade that darkens the valley
it shades your true intentions
covers those encircling
i just stand on this ridgetop
hand to the trees

head to the canopy
doth twin beauties
i walk
in muds i emerge
face in the west
a reflection of the dusk at dawn
celestial mirror

rest easy, old woods
i hold my PEACE fingers

to YOU

Saturn Sensorium

                    spinning fractals of dragonions
                      and scorpions and skullions!
spinning all confusing plaid
glowing sincerely
dark purple eyes heading to street

                    the sun is allowed to enter
                            what?
                        orange sphere
                        orange pyramid
            delicate thin lines turning yellow to gray

                      this makes no sense
                          changeling!

              cool pulsations of yellows and greens
                        BIRDS SING
                            who?

                                        earth silent evermore
                                              HOO HOO!

Cascade Vein of Dream

                                                                          spring winds
                                                    aerobic upwelling
                                                  river colder than sea
                                            alders greening leaves
                                            glassy reflective tonic
                                                      osprey hovering
                             startling ducks and cormorants
                                 having everybody dreaming
                                 of winter rain that never came
as i zoom toward fullmoon fortunes
                                   blasted by cigarette sand
                           in death's hot hangover of dawn

On the Other Side of Air

old jack frost,
old man wint wint
oh i am much like you

young woman hepcat pads past us
no, she says i am not this
i feel how and how now i slip a slow quote into my daily lone bliss —

you had the feeling of early-in-the-morning
like a hermit's joy*

—beatitude!

fan me all across your winey reddreams
unsheathe so we see from ridge hermitage and fly red-eyed
        to mama-moan-sea-ocean-bone

kerouac oh parker oh dizzy ode to the february fish fogs
keep thy deep driftboat morning mourn of steelhead water slaughters
washing in to join my mind of idle fast thoughtful miles

mysterious mists and quiet valleyheavenfrost fingernailing the way
to waves of haze and laughing loafing loaves of leaves
to foul of seafood rot bound wound to sweet oh sweetness cannabis cloud
fluff my fat cat face in futility

come noon i broomclaw and zimzoom out past the breaking pacific brains
ahoy yes jack,
still i can smell your cubans
from her cold gray seal salt womb
i can inhale your blue eyeballs
and that rainbow television set which watched you die all in our "common dark"

yes yes
your eyes are not open
do you forgive them?

old steve allen,
yeah, through the speakers in my black summer river car
i wheel toward watery wisdoms
yes, steve!
with jack he tickled ivories alongside forests
in that weird city studio of loose flies and neckties

onward they went
while i deepgazed into that barbyrust fishhook for that big dinner plate
in diesel deserts of stumps

old jack, listen
old jack, smell
fleet cork swarm
and you are forgiven
perhaps
in hell
for not answering those buddha parker eyes
slain by boozejugs and jug jugglers march '55

jack kerouac,
your ghost flies in my endless hungover morning mists
honeydew riffles in jade slant of sun,

flowers,
they sometimes pluck themselves
moments, they do weave into lockgolds of good
fat ford dodge chevy atop poor smashed river rock bars
cigarettes pout and pound amongst boat-trailer confusions

old jack,
a bottle is but a beginning
not?
pints of wine don't honor your moss mind
so here we can fall onto the golden phonograph spine of charlie
thy grand buddha of bop

drop a needle and follow his sweaty blackdrip line
to flaming orange annals of great america

blow! blow! blow! blow!

trail him down these old damp hills of fir branch in the plantation woods
in the ashy days as they drift by
the swooping hooded eyes of oatmeal earth

we stumble tumbledown yes
and with you we'll paw ourselves into large quantities of the holy grapey sea sun ship

jack!

where where will you go now?
drift into pastiche deaths of sun-dial roads?

no

for now it is our winter, like our own july gorge reveries
remember the river parker,
to the sea it blew three dead men

today, killing coastal rainbow trout
fulfillment without
paleosensual rainbow goddess
of my many nights deep in gold

so, jack, we a-go-go
swimming her wet ass-cheeks apart

*This poem is a paean to choruses 239-241 in Jack Kerouac's Mexico City Blues, Grove Press, 1959.

Serendipit

i hear you, strange bird
song in the mother tree
mother of three
hundred years

twisted shrouding meadow's web
no living thing
asked to be born
nobody
none of us

N
O
N
E

of our animal companions
but they choose to live
the world looks better in magenta
the world look better in violet
the world looks better than indigo
but lettus live in purple love

New Gale

oh cold oh fleet-feeting of sleeting
ragging in personal old gloom
oh bleak blackened
        bosom brow now
                                                of mother garden
        in monday heavyrain noon

high praise to your linear lidded ashen eye
        ferociously free-flying as a swirl-swollen banshee
sharp spine of earth will seduce this sweet new northwestern
        wetwild

fresh meditation levitation appointed to my zen precipice
        hissing through my old silent mountain fog
vaporous voids and
                                        ripping endlessly
                driving cloudbursts
belting screaming steaming cold
windows whistling
        electric air infiniting
                                                      come
                                          come stay awhile
                        enjoy our private timbered rising rivers of sky
                        let me howl into singsongs of dripping soils and
sooty memorial sunsets
                              while eons of orange splintered firewood
                                  settle snugly into my encharmed loins

supper:
cheese
salmon
olives
zinfandel and malbec

        "You are a lunatic"
                        says she

    says we another hour as it creeps through candlelight
    tomorrow will arrive somewhat madbrained upon today

lament in dead leaves and shut mercury eyes for now
                                                      not forever

                                                                just glance around

wind chill is piercing
                                          all usual drowsy indifference
windpipe of winged whiskers

                            and my beer-bellied bones await lonesome
                no!

        sparkling happy beaches of tuesday snow

Peace Tears
for Stephen Kew (1922-1989)

uncle sam duped
empire swooped
transpac sneak
        noise and metal thunder the skies of insanity
                death on the harbor, murder on psyche
                        day of infamy, sun of sickness
                                            raiding
weekend morn fleet and optimistic calms
raining bombs
and

hellwar   bullets
violence redux
                nine months on
enter fujita
fighter pilot in september heats
cocooned in oregon submarine

                    TORCH
                    THESE
                    WOODS
        grandfather,
                to where did age 20 pull you?
purple heart germany
fujita
                    grandfather would have beheaded you

            with your golden samurai sword of four hundred years

now a gift
an apology
honorary community member
preach practiced

hopeful youth redwood at trail's end
see you in a century

your bone ash nourishes our peace tree
O time does heal
your humbled eyes flew
now kneel to the lightning earth
i touch the serpentine soils

shared war tears
atop wheeler ridge, they

F
A
L
L

anew

Large Delicious

all of this will end in tears
primate emotions
primitive diversions
viscous brown historical foams
onto steep sharp slashing naughty knotty blackrocks laced-draped snowy white

our worlds pulverized by heavy four-thousand-mile wintergray trains
huge waterwalls of raw surprise
bolted wake in tickle of bearskinjuice
purr pounding
feel its foggy rumble

wavy warbly wobbly slowmotioning shake awake my deep gray thunder roll
tiny white gulls race race racing curls
teasing joy through sad unstoppable millennia of play
why stop?

because we spy the pinnacles of freedom
the soft warm black cat curls
the spit brown fury bellyroll dance madnesses

again of course she rolls,
and northwest horizon softens with new rain
gulls ultimate vibration, connection innate, deepest bind twixt flowing force
curls cold core expirations
the value of sin

sloshy!
curls!
and

S
O
A
R

air surfing
in spindrift heaving growling explosion grinding fades above fat-blasted
pastel soft-focus walls of lard flexing and long sea zen shatterings
by black sharp rude landform abruptions
washings of carnage on microscopic wings of free instinctual joy
raw baby strawberry vines wind-stunted
you sneaking sitkas into the groove

the gulls!
whitegray swoosh!
deepest engagement i have ever seen

raw primordial wall of young conifer where once sandy prairie once preened
wavy oceanspray ignores gravity
the sad drizzle
wash me
wash me again
scour the grains
oomph
oomph
searing thunderumble hollowecho
red sandstone skin scab pleasing the brown undulations
tiny red and hard orange worlds
a severe meeting

baby shorepine below the foggy bowl of salal
loud! rippingly roaring whitewater lunge over sad sea-palm
sharp white and misty fade
spent black dead mushroomheads refilled
with wet hopeful yellowgreen five-lobed miniatures

widow's peak and fairy beard
how much water have you breathed?
bashed into?
sloshed across?
sliced veins?

her primeval black natural bridge rock will reject you
her freak of time
rumble of urgency
blackybrow vertical foams
gulls—always
razor sharp beak and claw

i want you to ponder that messy collapse in the distance
bound to delicate fairy falls
the gray congeals and blends into
blackish white gray confusions and still on we march into drowning rocks
the air is a misty white

brilliant young needlegreens against ancient wet black rock-carved stream
look at that magnificent graygreen profusion haze!
all woods and wine, right?
there is not and no such
it is an uproarious glisten vision toward ancient ultimate earth evolution
have a sip of stout or sirah
haze on above the bushyhead
has been here forever
will be here forever
what is forever?

water

bend to me
collapse your primordials
airs of salt in mist
the air heaves
slosh up the black
never stops
fresh decade of bombast

gulls eye swells of eternity far-reaching past and forward of this homo sapiens fraud
how many new trees have you seen today?

      impaling needles always flashing the ocean exhaust
    sharp browning dead beds of branch like bristly sandpaper
  rowdy forward thrust suspensions of whitewater yellow needles
                        all wet
               come back in a century or twenty
                      in wonder

your comfort is not a notion blasted upon moons and tides and time
                and yet time is not time but a shallow human dimension
      heavy oozes starwide from torquing black chutes
                  moist with twenty seconds of japan spawn
browny-orange-beige-green baby sitka baby strawberry baby sedge
                               baby wondrous weed

                        BOOM

     these blacky-brown crags misty with newyear moods
                 newdecade dramas
purply black shiny shorepine root rain-wind-flares inside pure marine soup

        bury yourself in my emotion erosion
           melting mists and fogs creep
     wind feathers the loud green hedge of solitude
    bonsai sitka pressured-washed and suppressed
       pebbly bare shale like greenland
   windblasted lichen tundra of arctic temperateness
  fever playing stubborn with old raw black pinnacles

the slow silence with trains aligning to take turns and bash the ancient rock over
             dark depths explosions of white thunder
   eyeball mental rotoblade above i and i crouch amongst the dwarf woods
              tortured beauties of indian sands
                  of oceanic vertigo

   hear only the huge roaring thump and spent sigh of solitude

the deep rippling ripping thunder crack lichens and dewy micro salal
microshorepine and caterpillar ferns

old fungi with sad inverted cupped caps filled with blue algae and cold rain
footprints of deer and dog and human eroded
old and fresh in the rain-mottled brown sandcake sweeps and tiny black wet brook
delicate frilly falls flashing down the black rock skull of the ancients

whimsy of young shorepine tunnel trails of sand
scaly wet black barks of sitka congestion
delicious droopy gooey sticky wet sandstone
eventually
our tears will erode all of this magic kingqueendom

Hook Dreams on the Royal Road

"stick me in the gas chamber 'cause they've already taken my fuckin' life away"
      scowling pinching green garden hose with weathered skintips
donnie squirting decks of homemade fiberglass skiff erasing muds sands seaweeds
baby starfish
      detritus from another day nearshores combing fathoms sinking baited lines,
      aside donnie squatting in his homemade skiff,
bill with huge dungeness crabs clawing at the air,
      plucked from deep water a mile offshore
bill and donnie spent from aching long back-bashing hours,
      hashing hours
                baiting pulling fishing by hook-line
      method fast on its way toward sad gray sea death
"lawyer was down here just yesterday"
      donnie dudes through woolly irish-orange beard
"showed him all the paperwork and he said 'well, you're screwed!'"
      late sun warming my shoulders fatigued from my lingcod afternoon at sea
aluminum skiff buzzbuzzing from reef to reef talking to sea lions,
      "guys up on the hill still have salmon boats," says bill
"keepin' their permits hopin' they can go back to fishin' someday but"
"big dragnetters are the problem
      they control it,
          make the legislation,
              make the laws that control themselves,
                  they're runnin' us outta business"
                  two realities
      my skiff a toy at peace with seals cliffs white sharks
      bill and donnie skiffs aging sad lunks used for vintage chore
bill "bitch about it waitin' until they take it all wearin' us down...gonna quit one of these days but not till i have to. don't really know much else but i'll find something"
      find your poverty
         find your insanity
      find your drear and desolation upon happy rockshore of yore and your tired old blessings of abundance now dead and gone
      cannibalistic worlds
            killing,
                                                to be killed off

In My Blur

        squids as skeletons
      hammerheads as fleas
  pulsing tribal cartoon of prehistories
a cartoon of something we cannot understand
 mass autumn death coats all of our fat land

             in my blur

heads of snakes rise in the orangepink trees

             in my blur

    the weeds are gentle as lambs
       eager for wintersleep
returning to serve earth with kind beauty

to hear crunch of dead brown grass
    soft breeze floats over
      the bliss of bees
       listen to them
       around my feet

             in my blur

      sucking faces
   sucking from rocks
   sucking out of rocks
barfing like barnacles on the flash of earth
      a twinkly echo
        magenta
        tell me

what do your eyes smell?
what do your ears taste?
what do your teeth hear?

the earth is not settling
non-cycle
we are all living to die

each year is not a new us
no wisdom to vitality
no wisdom to not seeing the sun
feeling the grassy warmth
weed is a four-letter word
no such thing

in my blur

fluorescent pink glowy fields of weeds

happy feather love

bones falling to fat flowers of meat

Magnum Madrone

ping-ping-pow-pattly-rattly-rat-rat!
whipcracky-snappy-snap
pew-pew-pew!

sunday greetings
funday
greetings sunday
gunday

load 'em up and littercake those old dead dusty log road dirts
pulverized by sweaty age armies of whit-log trailerings and steely cat trackings
scuffed by greasy caulk boots and smelly two-stroke oils
cig butts and crunched silverlight cans of—

hey hey ain't no clouds today
hey go snow-gutter spit into all that vaporized harmony
go shatter that coast range reverie
raise a new sonic
sound bath reversal
deep deep into rudimentary freedom ranges
all within the free national forest range
actually not a real forest at all

from these free sunny marine vales they head on upriver and upridge
blasting projectiles and twelve-gauge rage
freewheeling pistols and rifles and revolving volvers,
pack-pack!
pew-pew!
letting relative isolation host the stage

spew more lonesome empty cartridges onto these shatter piles of spent shotshells
spit again into raw rusts of deafness and poisoned fades of aching clearcuts
yes yes, for the all-ringing white ears of angels in all hells

come on, let's leave our red casings for nature should she ever be allowed to reload
come on, let's know that the second amendment can never ever amend earth

come on, let's load wad-cutter hollowpoint roundnose lead and
full metal jacket

decomposing?

centerfire rimfire chetco bar fire
prairie to fir plantation to stump to spiky black widow
and so and so happy and hungry like a rolling dire wolf i prowl
on two fat tires
down along weedy crackly creeks and moody checkerboard canyons

then a-howling at once my ringing ears they come a-wrapped
in a symphonious shooting
a-swirling all 'round
oh like the whirling tired orange of autumn leaves

but not really

hey, everyone,
all sides unseen
don't blindly shoot toward this fluorescent orange hat
i'm gonna wheel this old heavy non-mountain bike on back up that foggy rock track
back to cats and snacks and yesyes to my very own hibernation
of soft gunpowders inside the world of bird-chirping ear-ring of
green precipice
stolen peace

Honeydew

later, above bear river,
feeble black vans climb huge back bellies of cow shit vistas and woods
tales from the dream guitar serenade me in the petroleum valley
approaching cannabis dews of honey
where the low mattole lazes in the sweet shimmer of midday wind
the scenic weathered barns,
horses below the raw green bulge in the famed greenvalley of rain,

winterdead cattle grids
mounds of moldy woodchips
winey mossy maples along terrible road in the slipstream
bending into the once-paranoid dust of the cannabis culture crown
honey hills select with furs,
road washouts
discreet growdozers transporting tears of terrestrial tranquility
fast quiet ranchlands of black steak
primal mailboxes reminding me of the gaunt old man
who waved at me on a yellow windy morning near the cape

bony fingerpalm from another era
cattle not cannabis
farms not firearms
small white pickup, sunshine smile

dead now—

the quaint friendly ranch wave
draining to round guts of fly fisherman beering at nine a.m.
between nursery pallets of giant soil dreams

and the slow lost raven souls who will meet at the honeydew store
agape for now
singing sweet of past and fore

Intellictivity

some of us humans get stuck in sad muddy dead-ends

while fresh fertile kaleidoscopes

swirl 'round and 'round

like infinite spotlights in space

plant symbiosis

they have always known everything

trees talking with each other

on your tombstone

old ode to fungi

Limbic Lightning

silver mirror mind fade
knife fade
spoon fade
fork fade
spork fade

greetings old whistling cold skin
old slick salami hands in primus stove crackerboxes
smearing waters of painterly skies
ferncreek splat
bombastic conifer highs

ongoing, so
go on?

switch sides on broken redwood firehouse wheelbarrow
smelling stupid busted bear balloons of bliss
buried shallow in the raw lonesome moon of fool

i see
mad dreams of burnt bodhidharma matchsticks
slapsticked all over greasy spit-gum alleyway walls

hoary doves and hello housecats,
dragging fat sticks of fertile frankincense
across low deserts of diseased dirt carpet log ponds
curating high-speed chases through clouds of confusion
clawing into elusive oily rainbow ridges of your wettest eden tea leaves

mind over manzanita, i say
enlightenment to fertilize, like these hard furious raindrops do
heating the corners
yet everything always,
always
just fade-fading away

just

dreaming now

weird childhood visionfaces that never occurred
adrift in humanspaces i never knew
in holyplaces i'd never seen
no cozy dark flashback ace sanitarium sheen

no,
no stroke of ambrosial goddess
as all of you are

sadness

ahoy still the rain falls, blessing the gut of galaxy
and still the lord trees a-swirl

never forget
never recall

slippery uncorked memories until we awaken
our mossy minds—

all

Mouthfish Mystic
for Dan

upon shivering pale pastel dawn cigarette-butt monday dirt
at weaving winchuck sunrise in sharp downstream airs
in mossy string-hanging redwood seams
seemingly where here, yes! there meets our kindred woolsocked feet

we understand this
firm warm handshake and stained coffeeteeth
thy toes they may numb
early eyes always atwinkle with promises of raw aching ocean

praises to mothers of trillions
considering mazes to droopy black plucking arcs
or to flat hard white glassbarks
here again, camouflaged wader legs and slick black rubber kneeboots

there again, heavy damp australian wetsuit and ancient californian waxbar
baldhead and beard and tidy old fishpole and gnashed tackle stashed deep in the red
borrowed stinky luke jeep
look down and kick
frigid clean dawn asphalt

ick!

the favored northeast wind it blows!
funnel rivers
gentle sky bluey-gray flecked with cotton candies of our chiseled lives
and as always we chase the low pressures
and we trail the window-whistle rhymes of autumn
those coastal crossing points

and this is yet but one of your long havens
wood plains east west north south dirt water sober hangover
your battered green toyota truck once bleeding from open-minded naked comic relief
once swinging dead lingcods in the saint patrick's day dusk
once lone ranches of merry first dips

now!
we cannot give to nature what nature gives to us
still!
we squint red-eyed into the ruffled new waters and the littoral pebblesands
of our mindful mutual sanctuary
rich in gull guano
smooth dingleberry rocks
rough absurd abused tranquil gray logs

all while the kalmiopsis blows its unknowing timber traffic into our early earholes
deaf to the shark-scared seals and lions
as you later reveal upon beers in brookings

                      hither hither fall chinook salmon
                              you said—
                      you man-threatened species!

                                you said—
                     they avoid your humble hopeful barb

                                          so let us praise the wet gears
                                        the core of atmospheric rivers
                                       the confluent cycles of currents
                                  the forty-six thousand drainage acres
                                                      because

                              LO!

the jewel rainriver at last has slit our old dormant foot-stepped summer beach
before and after i howled like a fool at huge ridgetop winds
and gray rainsmokes rushing through the tall firs
and my dormant rhododendrons and gleeful gray madrones and catnip

deep december voices that indeed drained away the sorrow of solitude
                            lunatic ecstasies engaged in grayblaze glasscreaking gustery

and so you hook nothing!

new normal

because, after all, happiness rides in the scorching yellow room beneath spindrifts
you knowingly will step through the scattered orphanwood coffins

you have been here before

                        intimate seasonings
                        forefather of respect
                    thank you for your inspirations
                    together we serenade this axis
                            blessed bees!

         so i will see you again upon the muscled seariver shore
                        mother will decide
                    and smiles we will provide
                              again
                            in waves
                            waves in
                              again

Horse Mountain

vega winks at me through secretive tanoak boughs—silent sky of shy last-quarter

libra moon lifts from the southeast in the king range heart night—while chill of

wee-hour sleet sinks deep into the holy unholy snowdrifts of zenmemory

Green Forest Capes

bradley and i leaky-tented here and there in the late rain and late fire and
always we blinked day eyes in cold late puddles of dry headache hate and
        late beerwine foul,

but first
always

came the cracked lips of briceland pinot noir and the old lodi petite sirah from
        greasy green glass grin bottles
and those longnecked browns of red nectar and the melodious rash of crickets and
        heartfelt oatmeal stouts and mystically twinkly frogs in the brush creek bogs

bradley—

do you remember those cold dewy keg ales from arcata?
and the purring creek waves that curve-wove the road
        westwarding one-o-one north to south?
indeed,
do you recall the frightening el niño blasts of black southwinds through mossy arced
        conifers of confusion?

hot woodsmoke buffeting mad spaces and sad faces in our humbug mountain night
loud surf in the ether hiding from your bhikkhu trance
and my sorry cold corpse of wetsuit
we hugged the torquing oranges and yellows that beamed immense prizes of peace
then skipped on south to the next secret cove

reveries in northwinds and gemlike green
glittering dune jewel in wind-shaped whitesands
windsurfers in world paradise

bradley—

do you recall our wildernesses of thought?
our whipgales around rockfaces?
zooming drunk rubber through dizzy redwoods and screaming from golden hilltops?

prying poor russian abalone from mendocino jug handles?
pissing into the salt wind at point arena?

bradley—

                      are you still subterranean,
                        snoring in your leaky tent,
               burning sai baba's famous nag champa?
                   in your calm cut of potter valley?

lost time and mind makes it easy to shatter the chromotherapy of my purple heart
    all too easy to wince from hyper hopes of wet verdurous youth

Nirvanas of Your Mind

        you, down there in your hooded pinks
                      alone
          swimming through waves of depression
                    thinking
                    nobody
                     would
                      ever
                      join
                      you

Flower Days

resinous green

sheeting

ubiquitous
continuous
monotonous
formless

floral rain sky cracks late for a tender bloodthin dusk
mirroring the yellow laser of sunrise
in the
cold damp gladness of december-end vortex

of neptune

upon your pillow of geovomit
beneath the whoring gulls
amid feasting of seal heads
secretive steelhead
slipping past red eyes above the red bud of earth
the rivermouth comforts me
no other place dies like this

General Ecstasies

greetings to our blessed riverine!
rushing roaring whoring past
your world fast and
FAT
graymudbrown beauty
uncoiled snake of
SEX
rocky riffles as white blurs
on downwest oceanflows
where late-season chinook thrash upstream
where steely steelhead steam
in dark seam watercaves of wealth
where crumbling riverbank muds
howl at our rude roadsides
where raw salmonberry vines
weave in the tremendous drench
of gnashing wishes
with trembling himalayan blackberry sugar armies
those great old death winterthorns
where mists windspewed upriver
from the sensually scented sea
splattering black dreams
onto mossy old fernytrunked myrtlewoods
glistening purple wall
of all sword ferns
and all huckleberry
groaning greenferns of fruit fancies
crowding the downed mossy logs of lucidity
and so
and so we walk
coldfaced shiny wet ferns slap our bare hairy skin shins
we roll in carpets of green clover
bushy where the ragged red cedars grow
deciduous alders stripped of summerspring
let us plod amongst them

do not disturb that quiet deer clan
with your clumsy splooshy footfalls
in the yellow-orange-brown
mother hymns
crack your spine and look up!
hammergray smashed sky sparks laser crowns
of bigleaf maple faces
all along the secret south bank
our river fordable until recent days
long months of light flow
now droughts of long memory
tiny societies of creeks tumbling loudly
to the veins of universe
down the capillary creekstreams in my eyes
waving amniotic air of spores and camphors
foundations in yellow slimes of banana-slug buds
COME! COME!
gaze deeply into the basements of these swirling eddies
these captive caged driftwoods
all bulged to well beyond the mecca
where we blissbathed that sunny osprey summer
sweating on hot hard gray cobbles
and smooth silken barbecue sands
amid fragrant dainty hopeful august weeds
the world naked in limp green whirly-whorls
sunburnt beers and confused bikini blings
lazy prismatic kayak floats
loose happy blisters of abandoned love
all for virgin halcyon memories
Y E T
again!
again!
again!
and
A
G A I N

Gossamer in Weep

stormswept hours
       whiskered chins dour
              diesel-sweat-meth power
                     quiet crustaceans cower
                            sandy seafloor scour
                                   cashmoney shower
                                         ecosystems deflower
                                               the ocean sour
    consider it ours

Babe Vibrations

presence of trees
sweeps my air
and babe vibrations of my insane pain

copper webs of manzanita
long wavy waves of purple grass
echoes of my empty people over in the raging valley

lettus regroup among limbs of gravity
our tentacles of time
and then not-yet adult brambleberry thorns
that live to prick you

new life from the old stump
all dying is all beginning
the man is dying
the earth is growing
with every death is a birth
rainbow of life

rainbow holes and valleys droopy
my faces in the livewire boughs
slow-motion with the drops quivering loopy
blowsy dandelions aside creeping cats

Empryean Odyssey

one white gull
glides

                    low across wind-brushed
                    bluey-green sunny dawn surfs
                    above seals and below incense arcs
                        of rainbow spindrift

two black ravens
burp

                    and quibble below december cirrus
                      above crowns of stained firs
                    homeless in secret mossy streams
                    hollows where waterfalls bicker and
                    steelhead pools where sad suns dream

three brown owls
prowl

                    swivelheaded branch busts
                    sharp streaks in smooth river sky
                    deep in the holy holy dims
                    of yesteryear's forest night
                        never forget
                    my sneezing stag and farting bear

four gray quail
brood

                    hermetic fairy spirits
                    blessings of my dead feathered nymphs
                        hairy tongues
                    buzzvisions of six summer wasps
                    salty gristle of constipated earth

                                                take me AWAY
                                                    hunt me up
                                                  hunt me down

                    O
        sweetened blue honey talons!

                        i
                       wish
                        i
                       was
                       you

Glimpse Dream Eden

my sister suggests a cranial skull exam of loose format
wrapped in a carry-out box of toxic plastic

                                    hours later,
        greg and i flow frigid greens between blaring rise and bowling set
                snow-moony face-off with pure low dawn blast
                        squint into the glare
                        and recall surf sanity

Fade of Betelgeuse

"wines they await"
look!
it is mystic water

orion, i see you
tripping over shallow ferns
to reach babe times you will never see
stuck in your loud boots of china virus

angled in from heavy backpack of zinfandel
after your swing shift at the mill
studying dusty video games and tousled tarot cards

in essence, sure, we bob and weave to the sutras
go on
wait a few months for the color
for the shimmer
for the muddy ground rainbows full of wineywine fruit

Elk Creek Wash

                         and here comes nightfall
                         eternal nature of dream
                         mandala of thick thought

humans stuck in sad muddy dead-ends
while fresh kaleidoscopes swirl 'round and 'round
like the infinite magnet eyes of space

drunken supplications always are spit
green ratios, dead ratios
crying goodbyes to siblings
where were they going? where was i? do we wait?

i see a covert poetry reading occasion in a cluttered city coffee shop
jamie slouched detached wine-sopped
greasy white tables covered by empty used colorful plastic cups
all brown dregs at bottoms of hopes

                                  i blink
                               walk and piss

petrichor air and fungal ecosystems
holding court
urgent
and confounding

                                           now i saw elsewhere
                                    people i saw but never had
                                           cheshire grins
                          and then, wee hours of great delusion

orange tommy the cat sleeps breathing sounding like a tiny faint distant jet
the earth wakens to another vague windy dawn
stormy lesions, friends from the south
atmospheric rivers bleed to hermitage freshwaters
blessing the feed

and so
light floods the holy valley
blue iron gate
shattered red bong
smashed faded vial of visine
homeless hand of rain-soaked garbage
scattered down clearcut streambeds

                        green tiny polite deer fern maidenhair fern
                                         rainfresh falls
                          rushing to secret fairy redwood grove
                              secret scenty myrtlewoods
                            flowy lovely hemlock pyramids
                                  new wind snags on the trail
                                impassable but for chainsaw

and even more redwoods aside stony drainages
fed by alien aluminum culverts
astride the bike quivering down loggers gravel rattle
flanked by a million burnt stumps
and little naked hopeful creeks
spontaneous sophistications
for centuries natural and happyshade hidden
exposed now to the oily eyes of chokers and tweakers

                    sudden racket of gravity's water
                    from ridge to riffle to oceanic reef

                      nature washes itself of you
                        bushy redwood flanks
                    trunks slashed blue spray paint

targets of the intuitive old fella in the gray dodge diesel
this morning he says to me
'hey kiddo orange hat great idea,
stand out from them drunk deer and bear'

indeed soon cracking creep of unseen cougar watching my whiskers
then, hours later, a pretty young blond in camo jacket in red pickup
weaving north
i mime 'join me'
she waves, warm, smirking
heady pity in the mad wet wild winter day

my friends are sagacious salamanders and nubile newts
all left behind careless priority minds
silences of birds and hibernations
boom bust bust boom graysky dirts of doom all around
packed and poisoned
but only for dirtrose face of dormant rhododendron and lupine
leapfrogging foxglove
salmonberry wine soon

> i enter and i exit under the guise of wonder
> finding north of norm past the harvest boundaries
> where fewer know of anything and few forget
> and everyone else will never know
> whored waiting rooms of wilderness

Crystaldrip Camp

					let thy dreams sail doth thy fabric soaring torn
				 whet thy edge, splash thy soul, heal thy heartbeat
			thy wind whiffs for one, thy wishingness for wanderlust
																		yes

					blue fires of thy wet eternal indigo earth

forestRe

      young choker setter out on the muddy skid road glade
          says he's proud of his old generational trade
      indeed indeed gazing down upon these brown fades
        all in these moonfields of once-crystalline jade

        young timber bucker at waterside seafood bar
        tells me in a dream he sees seas of cuban cigars
     with his fingerdust from them erstwhile prairies afar
         says to me, 'i ain't never had no cookie jar'

young timber faller hey modern mechanization working against you
      in a dusk gold beach pub it was all brew and beef chew
he browngrins to me 'maybe i grow old and this be all i ever knew'
      shallowly i again think of tomorrow in green blue blue

Diesel Honey

fifty tons
forty-foot sticks

wheeled on down
oil-rolled arcanity

feller-buncher
harvester-processor
stinger-steer

to

terrifying sawmill
pulpmill
plywoodmill
chip van truck
china
home depot
sudden oak death

where is the end?
we'll get there
somehow
and die
reborn as sawdust

Drip Meditation

look look look, oh look
at our wholesome white pinhole in the great cassiopeiac teardrop sky
heaven is squawking at us
stand firm on the water 'else i breathe those heaving gray fogs
snow slaves to radiation of deer and the winged ones and polite noon gravities
flattened hidden brambles and foxglove rosettes and swirls of barbed wire rust

fall forward into the heavy wet
and frozen bubble toes
mound of broken branch
vertical white comets they may a-plunge
mercy! mercy!
vertical reverie behind the mystic harsh sitka beach
western red cedar and doug fir in stacks
broken tanoaks and manzanita madrone, halls miles upon lonesome miles
taste the sausage and smoked salmon and the green garlics
that hot woodfired coffee of witches
stitches between vivid solar reflect and stern flat steel-pan skies
and promising pregnancy like a dancing spring doe
simple energies urging me to freeze feet avoiding dump-thump of branch avalanche

in silent wistful snowfall i awaken to the old folk croak of dylan delivering truths
howling about hardfalling rains and blue-eyed sons and twelve misty mountains
hoopy tambourine men and hurricane boxer winds
they are a-blowin'—
—answers to me today,
tiny twinkled angels of aromatherapeutic atmospheres,
precious crispness of bluey-white chill, settling in densities,
truth-wrapping my weighted worm mind

silent white static
silent white winter, storybook meadow of huge-hipped firs
prescient realization wielding rare ranch glaring in gray
delicate quail tracks from tree-welling tapping secret pedospheres
weeping on down to secret salmonid holes
sleeping, dreaming inside the secret lives of rainbows

Etherealove

look at you
just look at you
an absolute pad of gold
how lucky we are to have
how little we know of
yeah we all know of you
here in the shadows
in the shade
never once beneath your beauty
your staff shafts of sunlight beating into the earth below
heated from the herculean heavens of volcanic

B
L
I
S
S

Dusk Murmur

on island earth i lay mesmerized
by millions of carpenters in the mother fir
from behind it creeps my dear waxing crescent moon
thick rough alert branches framing it just so
pushing it toward the late sun

listen, listen
the first timid night crickets

testing, testing
dusk a meditation of all hum

pulse
crack
chirp
buzz
swish
yick

all 'round the world's quivering wheel
metronome of birdsong and the day's perversion
the moon always oversees somewhere
around its orbits and views from alien bodies

birds

rubbing

popping

squishing

as a hawk flaps by i can feel its focus
his or her at the one little dandelion
left catching the sun's last race
thousand to see rises from the sea

      where is dawn now?

     i wish for some clouds
                             to paint the dripping light
          of chetco's dusk
                                 skies of spotted pink
huge firs pushing the moonrise west
                        instantly the scent of night awakens
        the dews, the mists
                                   start to settle
    the crickets and the gnats anew
                  sounds as one last daybird sweeps

wings curl over the last orange dagger of dusk

Featheries

        the
        rain
        ITSELF
        sounds
        like surf

        C
        H
        E
        W
        Y

tinfoil
crackle of drips
and windy *hissssss*
undulate from hand-clap
to interstate speed
whoosh!
of log trucks punching
through the storm
pressure-cooked muffle of northwestern whims

dying as slaves to short minds

Five Wick Wick Wick Wick Wick

five candles flick nervous shadows across the walls and ceiling
the fog thins and thickens but never lifts
the fog in my battered drinking brain

in the meadowlong gray i smell't the sea
drooping fallow fat fields of fury
meadows of meander

Mellifluous Copulations

    we are all pieces

                      cumulative
                      of slutty stardust
                      to become ether

                      in between
                      suffer and decline
                      we try to rest in peaces

                      do we?

bliss
of the
big sleep

        (sleep forever)

Cassiopeia's Lullaby

in my old river cabin
she
was
the
one
constellation

as i lay
i could see
from the corner
of my cold cobwebbed dirty bed window

my most aloof lover
vain astral companion
we spun and spun and spun and spun

how dazzlingly buxomy vaingloriously of her to
dream over me each of those clear cold waterside nights
where i wished i lived in a glass house

i wonder if she thinks of me now

WHAT EGO!

Cyclobullience

silence!
black coffee
oceanface glass velvet meditation
silent morning tickling snows of coast range
polite tender delicate flakes upon the heels of autumn heats
oranges of madrone slicked graywet
reds of manzanita blackwet

atmospheric pressure drop
secretive eye creeps and whirls landward
awakening boughs of fir and cedar

snowflakes vertical then tilt and flip
spiral galaxies
raw spinning furious hook of cloud rage
cyclonic eye
another spiral galaxy
confused fattening snow
ramping wind—
—frantic limbs

outside all grays and blacks and dull greens
a grayout!
brown and orange autumn leaves fly for their final death
slaves to the gale
terrors of gusts
roaring and scouring
peaks and plains of stormsong

screaming to me
whistling echoing deafening hiss of fright
deep thrum of tense roaring gale gusts
fuzzy fogs and mists of opacity
firs of fright
glossy loud monotone whisper
intervals of urgency

secrets of atmospheric alchemy
rowdy urgent tinkly flashing snaredrumrolls
aggressive sharp whipping stabbing rattling lashing soaking rain
alders molest young firs above the friendly huddled brambles
and ferny ferns above the storm stream

obedient trees
i love you
rushing rivers of hyper cloudwind
rolling waves
pulsing sighs and weeps and roars

burrowed in all blizzard of alaskan birth
the blinding billowing cloudfog
blasting shrieks through forest slits
an eruption
an abruption
greased gray gaps up the coast slopes
scalping ridgetop saddle of horizontal rains
dead twig stab me
dead leaf shield my eyes

rippling tapping bullet shredding rattling raw
broken glass chainsaw layers of shatterclack rain
rain rain rain yell at me!
louder softer louder loud LOUD
rapid rowdyfire
bombogenesis

trees lurch and stretch
slippery branches drunkenly nod and wobble
saying yes
no

are we drunk?
scotch whisky and chicken soup

Cry, Cry, Riverbloodingpool

herewith below wet southwind of january morn
holy rivermouth tarred and smothered
yanked to submission by huge boulders plopped

and so i kneel and i sink a forefingertip into cold muds of pain
into waxing crescent blood moon

                                    chet-zut
                    once prism to intact river jewels
                         naget-khe'tun, north
               now beer-belly blanched asphyxiate echo
                              tcet-xo, south
                 stuffed into wood ships at port orford
                                     or
                                  murdered
                   starved marched mostly naked
             along cold wintercoast trail of tears

canoe paddlers clam diggers dip-net bow arrows quiver spearer harpoon gaffers
woodpecker scalpers
albino deerskinners
all for tooth shells as money

aswirl in this stinking spread,
clang of restless sailless masts
        sugar shadows of fish canneryism
airs plugged with stacked bins,
ilwaco fish co stenciled on abdomens
              behind evil gnarls of barbed wires clogged with dead brown ivies
above freshly mowed little green lawns and tidy riverrock cusps of mnemonic space

remembrance honoring murder and greed in 21st-century sheen
indeed,
pebbly port paradise of rust and saliva and shattered glass
sad wail of that old cold lonesome whistle buoy
rills of brown polluted boat basins and cold mists

wanton rains
over defeated brows of breakfast

fogspace crease of fish industry squalor bred forests of crab pots
of mildew and black dust
and diesel pickups burping and farting past this graveyard of boats and great hopes
        and holy tendersome athapaskan hearts

today one orb of concrete
163 years to build
replicas of milled cedar and colorful paints
planked slabbed semi-subterranean half-dirtmerged dwellings of cedar
        split by elkhorn wedges driven by stone mauls
stone firepit on dirt floor center
two-pitched roof
hole for doorway, enter/exit feet first
hunting for salmon smelt deer elk seals ducks sea lions ('ocean deer')
gathering roots berries bulbs seaweed shellfish acorns from tanoak
acorn bread baked in heated sands
chetco butter (deer tallow salmon grease)

                      (not now)

      of colorful informative rain-drip placards and guano-splashed planters
        of oregon grape and strawberryhuckleberry and a zillion bark chips
                snuffering the wheezy indian earth
                      ruthless rebar

ah yes you old bummy shipyard of fool
where shaggy feral cats rule and the soupy air blows rust and salt across the creaking
        metal boardwalks of burnt brains,
where dozens of shiny white fish-killer hulls and small pleasure sails await the sweets
        of banana-belt summer
where white rotgut mobile homes loom above a once noble kiss of river 'twixt sea,
where the bones are quicklypicked clean

moangroan gates and undulating steelslips swing-grind against forever winter of
    chet-zut discontent,
boat trailers and arrowtip light poles,
fine resting spots for arkbark sea lions and white-shriek gulls
doggy pinnipeds and aviary surf fairies
oh i do love thee

many many lats and longs away we see it to be australia day
bogusity invasion day
down under the fire sky squinting scuffed with incurable hangovers of genocide
aboriginal oh torres strait
athapaskan deepfeeling you

        and yet back here, up! up i look
            settler eyes
octo-inking pools of cloud settling on fuzzing cracks of blue

      my heart it sinks to the bottom of of the world
   my mind clangs like the flagless flagpoles beating the ocean air,
        invading the vague scenic roar of surf,
  barking sea lions, barking dogs, barking breach of sacred beach

        bad omens—hoot of owl cry of bobcat
           ceremonial rocks
            thunder rocks
      talking rocks, hailing chiefs to meet

              (now)

        tiny weeds pierce tiny cracks,
       tiny wildlife tiny ancient seeds
         recurring and hopeful

vast potholded puddled parking lots for dumpsters
          slippery boardwalk
  old weatherbeaten coffee shops and liquor store

hair salon and ice cream cones,
tourist kitsch for hire,
saltwater taffy,
clam chowder fish and chips
expensive but delicious pizzas
and dive bars of smoky gloom where bartenders are strippers
and nobody enters except the drunken morning pains of age and endless vietnam
      wars and ills of aquatic exploit

spirit tide salmon eagle bear wolf deities
salmon running,
ultimate sacrifice to support mankind
bones washed downstream and reassembled and repeat

squint into the bowling mists of the river valley and the swooping arc of bridge
contemplate seasonal villages for food gathering and shamanism
from misletni (mislatnah) to mother sea
between shattered towns of fungus humanity
above desperate salmonids and froggy muds of oil rainbows and cigarette butts,
plastic bits and sad trashes speared in eddies along naked aldercottonmyrtlebanks

somber i sit eyeing sad winter docks and old brokendownward flats hung high on the
      estuary abused north bank,
where drugs and diesel and desultories intermingle to the cry of buoy
and downheavy rains of despair

                                                indian wars
                                                          oh,
                    been crying pondering it all through
                                      dear chetco
                                            in just two
                                of thousands of years
                                       my unholy kind

          wholly deleted you

Kitty Creek

quaint fern rainbrook raising
moon shining white fog in the redwood night
                gently it pries apart my yellow radar fingers of sun

hairy day, it tumbles
lethargy and long illness and
large insurmountable seas speaking to me up the creek
tumultuous torn sleeps on wine-dark sateen sheets
i am january-coughing and blowing and twisting torn in tormented dreams

the lifting day has no name
each falling night is the same
thousands of misty dawn coffees truly mundane
and so there come aims of abundant green oxygen
                                            again
                                                i mesh
with the winding ridgeback road of sharp quick greed
tiny black gravel grinding black rubber
you look across to bearded buttes and those stripped mad scalped mountain brows
to brown scorched prairies of gunshot
to those not-so-distant perfectly friendly snowcapped easternwild blades

humming ceiling of gray shades the windowless homeless old yellow van
and its old smelly loud generator at noon
parked on this pesticide herbicide emergency brake
long sad wet squares of quarantined fir farms
sprinkled with trash and dirtbike ruts
                                      secret soft steep brown trails
tremendous ancient rotten stumps and cougar caves
weeping recycled ecosystems of shattered mushrooms
ominous pink tape and spray-painted bark
                digits of death and noise and of splintered gloom
the angelic air is much colder now
the blue gate keeps you away
silent thoughts on liberty of legs

Boughs That Blind

                              celestial sensorium
                              clouds of beneficence
                         breeding skies of inverted oceans
                   orgasming soft silent falling angels of frost
                            hazy graywhite celestial bliss
                                        air of felt
                                          until
                                        vanishing
                              into black fire of wet earth
                                onto sad fir stumps

                                         naked

                                     open wounds
                                       sap tears
                                      crying rings
                                    decades exposed
                                     arbor agnosia
                       capturing decades of these falling angels
                  from black fire saved by bold crown and sweet bough
                                clouds again soon crack
                             creep south to bless other universes
                          wakes of romantic pulsing finality of light

Bathluminous

shhhhhhhhhhh!
HUSH
windriver
sunriver
sleet
river
snowriverrush

oh holy holy riverwind!
undress my cosmic radiant point
not this year,
puppis!
vela!
needles will make you constellations listen
venus, jupiter, saturn

cold hot balls
i am sorry
dismiss the chainsaw and the body odor
choke on friday burnpile bluegraysmokes

we gullies gag
we canyons cough
we wildlife WHEEZE
but look!
listen!
crack your neck

S
Q
U
E
E
Z
E

your gravities
this raw ceiling of us wants to cry

we have fancy prancing dancing leaves
brittle whistling old black screens
a dripping ballet of browns to greens

shhhhhhhhhh!

tap tap tap tap tap tap
pitterpatterpoppopopwhooshwhooshwhoosh

oh dear you, dark dark wet wet sky
blinding me with your subjectives and convectives
let us wine/whine
goodnicenight
and let your ball begin

Velvet Stardust

listen!
honor what is
and
LET THAT CAT SCRATCH THAT FENCE POST

let modern uneven wavy gray rings
wander around their hard woven eye of age
let thorns nest themselves in the drought
while jumbled hard octopus limbs lay

D
E
A
D

in
the
hopeful huckleberries of heaven

my bristly bed of savvy swordferns
sharp orange rocks stepping on me
piercing my bark
taking your evil screeching chainsaw
to slash and sever my smile
headache me from slumber
feed me pickled raven eggs

PLEASE
burn your abused spider roots
in your dead poison-soaked soils
your raped cones and broken needles
please burn your next dry pile of myopia
the result of your sustainable ignorance
burn the earth at both ends
freeze that brown vile smoke
into the free ecstasies of cloud

it smells of dust drought death
and 170-year war against earth

spherical whore of maniacal meatheads
echo your ammo across canyons
stupid bullets in the gunfires of weekday morn
minds of endless flat dead-end discs
guns and beer and boredom
doldrums of distant bark dogs

finally the cougar trots to the peaceful red barn
LISTEN
ding!ding!ding!ding!ding!ding!ding!ding!

ICE -STAINED RUST-BELL OF FREEDOM RINGS

Candle Magick

your clean crooked prisms begin their colordance
over the black wet oregon night
none of this means nothing
to my fraying crooked eye-lens fringe
eyescanning your gray wet wooded hollows
your noisy birded green valleys
these things are all much much clearer
to the heart of a meat beat
a floating honey sense
a hard nation
gazing above soils into those mess of people
yes we may float along with me
in july you would always gasp with me
in august please puke with me
on harvest moon please hangover with me
in october please fart with me
in november please vote with me
in december please die with me

Babbling Nightbrook of Lady Triptych

                    inverted elk drawn to dewy dawn sedge and pattertap rain
           as polite dusky-footed woodrats bed down for the sure doom of day
                          i alongside young catlike gaptoothed smiling girl
                            whose van woke me in a gyppo yeasthaze
                                  she here all the way from okiehoma

                                            no—not you

                        elissa, heidi—do your memories fall on any of this?
                              lazing drifts in those early autumn wists?
                  our windswept grasslands at the stead of old frank mckee
                            he here all the way from irie iowa sunny

                                      we drifted about
                                        all amongst
                       tanoak limbs and our entwined tan limbs
  sugar innocence massaged by ecstasy in visitations of candor and curiosity
         of cameras and contemplations and of corinthian content
                              this was all a time—yes?

                     a time now historic as 19th-century apples
as amongst oldgrowth abundance of madrone and baffling douglasfir mutations
                            that historic mckee apple orchard
                           that sweet mountain valley prairie
                             those mystery mistdrip woods
                        there falls a dew over my irises
                                      indeed

                                              yes,
                            i would do again and aghast
                                      at last

                blast heavily into our twelve-point past

Zoom To Moon

drumrolling snareglass glassy rainrattle
over my foggy soggy rain head
never understate your silver self
we've all been here before

                      cool amber islay liquid in my clear bulb of glencairn
                      oil glassine corners in holy foreshadow of midnight snows
                                        the lazing trees of green
                                          the hazing static of gray
                                          optimism breeds fantasy

ruddy sun islands in elevator flows
dark square gutterplastic pissing
ribbed black piping directing vibrant wetnesses
dripping before your stained white bark of quarantine disease
wet and dead or dying as all of everything ever was and is

            the lulls in theory suspend like wind while it picks its pathways to paradise
                                  urging flexibility to adapt and embrace
                                                          never fighting
                                                       never resisting
                                          honoring what is evermore

crackling orange woodstove heat
curious cats all 'round
warm winey beef stew massages my winterbeaten belly
no place i would ever be
storm be kind as you always are to me

                      your cloud light brightens and darkens to damper dims
                              my brain suspended in the silence between suites
                  pondering future jazz free upon every football given sunday

reach out and out for that green glass bottle of nectar
impossible without eonic waters for miles of thousand
cosmologics indeed will breed purity for modern convenience

                                                        boatloads of boozy bliss
                                                          land upon that far shore
                  eleven years since i fell deep and wise to your peaty charms
                          and fell in love with boho-chic hippie vixens of eden

which is eve
which is anywhere
which is the heaven,

                      the heaven of your sentient present

Aurora

                        time your return to the body

                             intellective existentialism
                                unleash perceptions
                   mystificate your rivers of consciousness
                              your eyelids of stones
                              move in to move out
be with to be well

                                                                time is space
time your space

                                         brainstem vertebraic countdown
die now

                                                                live later?

King Peak Perseus

flapping through pungent schemes of rhythmic tinnitus dreams
restless depressed sleeps in greasy shivers of newmoon time

    and bear creek campsite doldrums in rinds of promise and old praise of budding
    youth moaning and wee-hour wonder-beaming 'bout what my life lonesome is a-
                                                                                                              doing

why i am from? why i am going?
screaming from societal stews in the skipping tao heartpulse
        of these sunken red wrinkle-skin eyes

darkness draped quickly its cold wings 'cross arcata
so with organic humboldt wines i rattle and bang up wash-rut rubble spines
        into sadfaced anxiety of drought disorder
into petite sirah of solace
the winter of king range content [con-*tent*, not *con*-tent]

            where mermaid fantasy of pacific sweat starts to startle (forest) birds
              where through woe i creep twixt cozy holes of chaparral and salal
                                                                                                                     mesmerized
                                                                              by huge fireblack ghosts
                    with longviews of honeydew valley in quiet sundays of sight

i massage and kiss the rough blackbark
fingertip and cheekface the mini turkey tails
awaiting all the rains of desolation

i complement the hopeful new bushy tanoaks in stern fire scars
petrification perfection
infused with the gentle sugar of bloody manzanita bones amid orange madrone

        and tangled roots of hope to the gurgling creekfalls hidden from man,
        a flirting descent in the steep slopes before the infinity of fir cones fall on me

finally with the rain of the februarian magick
the bowl of flames and firs quiet as dust in this second third of winter

sudden windgusts like gunshots boil up to the battered peak in the shade of moss,
and my mind mumbles with jazz kerouac monk talk—

thelonious, he was so weird he wandered the twilight streets of harlem in winter with no hat on his hair, sweating, blowing fog—in his head he heard it all ringing*

i me myself pierce the blowing fogs of hairy armpit mermaid sweats
and later the beige alluvial eden of big flat sweeps its big fat finger between the fogs
        four thousand blinks below

i thin my eyes amid this skygaze of past reveries
in drizzling calms of the winter world
wet caress of meditations and incantations and drip murmurings

all of this sinks upon the bristling windy lip of high southwest humboldt earth
whose grandeur shrinks the ego with the hush of its huckleberries
and where the cold northwind, it sings of the sea
like the viral blue snows of self-exile
and the damp damp damp pregnancies of lightning time

**From "History of Bop"*—Readings by Jack Kerouac On the Beat Generation, *Verve Records*, 1960

Dreamwood Meridian

mattole headwater starry night yanked dank blank
to starbuck to reveal drizzle-dead heads of deer
later to lick legions of large lithe water liters
gleaned in all greenblack tanks in deep solar panel passionfart privations
always off-grid against on-grid
or is it with—grid?
yes!
each will grease each
white market, black market
into the mumdrum we see as salmon sea
won't last
and neither will we
dive that deep end of ends
and decades on
and still you carcreep pass clusteryards of bashbusted acned buddhabuses
and laughing molds
in your parents' noble soggy whitethorn desolation
in their huge wet redwood stump hangover of gopherville
granddad's ghosts of lumber camps
mama miracles of monastery
cannachampion chimneysmoking drizzling wintermorning whalegulch road
yes newly it is all paved!
like life
please sign here
like your winding fourcorner reveries in the world of language
digging sweet sweet sense,
removing raw needlerock roots,
and tinklesawing piano keys into itchscalps of want
into eternal lungpulse your children will waltz
praise be to permanent muds of the usalroad log firework lust
praise be to the strata of cellserenity
praise be to endless intellect of nature

Tcet-xo, 2020

MICHAEL H. KEW first tapped his writerly destiny as a boy in the mid-1980s. His work has been featured worldwide in magazines, newspapers, films, websites, advertisements, and books, including 2012's *Crossings*, his first collection of travel essays. *Rainbownesia*, Kew's Oceania travel volume, was published in 2019. *Nectars of Sky*, his premier poetry collection, is based on his transformative residencies, precisely 20 years apart, along California's Lost Coast and Oregon's Chetco Coast.

www.ingramcontent.com/pod-product-compliance
Lightning Source LLC
Chambersburg PA
CBHW031309060426
42444CB00033B/993